T0095189

Old Men,
Pregnant Women,
Little Children
and
Beautiful White
Horses

Corinne Martin Rico't

iUniverse, Inc.
Bloomington

Old Men, Pregnant Women, Little Children and Beautiful White Horses

iUniverse books may be ordered through booksellers or by contacting:

iUniverse
1663 Liberty Drive
Bloomington, IN 47403
www.iuniverse.com
1-800-Authors (1-800-288-4677)

ISBN: 978-1-4502-7590-3 (sc)
ISBN: 978-1-4502-7591-0 (ebk)

Printed in the United States of America

iUniverse rev. date: 2/9/2011

Contents

Korean War Fighter Pilot Songs

Lady in Red
Air Force 801 (Itazuke Tower)
Boozin' Buddies
You Can Tell a Fighter Pilot
Korean Waterfall (Oh Death, Where Is Thy Sting?)
Bless 'Em All
Throw a Nickel on the Grass

To J Boy, your Daddy loved you so;
and To all our beautiful grandchildren and great-grandchildren

Preface

I have had this book in my head for a very long time. I have written paragraphs and chapters for years, but now at the urging of family and friends—reminding me that time is passing—I have organized my recollections into this book. This story is just a year in my life as I remember it. I have not researched times and dates nor events. These experiences are my memories and my life as I experienced it.

During one of my earlier writing modes, when I asked Jack if I should use his real name or a pseudonym, he quickly replied, "Call me Sam Hawk, I've always wanted to be Sam Hawk." And so Sam Hawk he is. Since I have changed his name, I thought it only fair to change the names of all the others mentioned, to protect the innocent and the not so innocent.

My dear aunt Kathryn Martin, to whom I wrote consistently while in Japan, passed away in 2000. While going through her things I found a folder marked Corinne Rico't (Korean War). This folder contained many letters that I had written during my year in Japan. Bless her; this enabled me to remember events I had forgotten. I have chosen to include some of the letters in this book. I have deleted personal paragraphs and used those parts which showed the thoughts and feelings of an eighteen-year-old wife living in a war zone. I am eternally grateful to her for keeping this record of a little bit of history.

Acknowledgments

Several years ago, when I finally decided once again to write this book, my granddaughter Amanda Ames took scraps of paper and pages of scribble, all full of typos galore. She patiently deciphered and guessed a lot, but after a year or so got it all on her computer. Without her perseverance this book would never have happened. Thank you, Amanda.

One day I asked my great friend Anne Bowbeer, whose literary opinion I value, if she would read my manuscript and critique it. From that day on Anne has been my editor, computer communicator, researcher, email address, my eyes, and most of all, my friend.

Another dear friend and business partner, Nelda Lee, helped me through some dark days. One of the remedies she suggested was starting back on my book. Some days, when I should have been working, I was typing; then I would throw those pages away and type some more. Nelda was a constant in my life in those uncertain days.

My friends Debra and Ronald Anderson, graciously agreed to proofread my book.

There are many more family members and friends who helped and encouraged me along the way. No one accomplishes anything in life by herself.

The songs I quote are US Air Force traditional and in the public domain. The words are Korean War versions—as I remember singing them—of arrangements used by permission of Dick Jonas, <u>www.erosonic.com</u>. Jonas was a fighter pilot in the 80th Fighter Squadron in Korea, 1983-84. Dick Jonas also unselfishly answered questions and suggested leads to other sources. Bill McChrystal wrote "Air Force 801" ("Itazuke Tower"). Many of these songs originated in World War I; they, and others from later wars, have been chronicled by C.W. "Bill" Getz in *The Wild Blue Yonder: Songs of the Air Force.*

1. Sunset Limited

I, a woman-child clad in an unfamiliar maternity smock, stared out the window of the Sunset Limited as it sped past the hills covered with the beautiful bluebonnets of my native south Texas. I watched the familiar hill country turn into the unending flatland of west Texas, where the parched earth never seems to meet the huge blue sky. Large tumbleweeds rolled and danced among the big iron forks that pulled rich black gold from the vast land. Suddenly, rocks in magnificent formations jutted from the earth and slowly became mountains that one could almost see through.

If I were an artist, I would paint these mountains as purple glass. As the sun set over the distant snow-capped mountains, the ground took on a beautiful hue of pastel colors, and a gentle wind moved the earth rainbow at will. As I continued to gaze out the window, darkness fell over the outside world. The shrill whine of steel on steel as the train sped along the tracks seemed to be repeating over and over, "Where are you going? What are you doing? Where are you going? What are you doing?"

How did I, Carrie Mackey, from San Antonio, Texas, find myself eighteen and pregnant, rushing miles from home across an ocean to meet a man I hardly remembered? I was the only child of Millie and Ernie Mackey—a happy child with doting parents and grandparents and a large, close, extended family. At fourteen, my life changed forever: Millie died and left a hole in our lives. Ernie was grief-stricken and unable to take on the responsibility of a teenage daughter. I became a guest in the homes of well-meaning, loving family members. They all loved me and wanted the best for me, but no matter how kind and loving, they were an established family, and I was an outsider. My still-grieving father and I, a rebellious teenager, made several attempts to make a home together; but finally he rented a room for me near my high school with a "fine, Christian lady," who turned out to be a tobacco-chewing, spitting, frustrated woman.

Into this lonely existence came an exciting, handsome young man who dared to fly jet fighter airplanes. Sam Hawk had a jaunty walk and a confident shrug of shoulder that convinced me everything would be all right, and life is good. We fell in love, and made plans to marry. My dad and family were horrified; not only was I too young, but Sam was a Yankee!

We married at Williams Air Force Base, Chandler, Arizona. Even though the air force discouraged aviation cadets from marrying, we had a double wedding ceremony with Sally and Larry Geropolis, another young couple who wanted to be together. The base chaplain pronounced us men and wives. The brief ceremony completed, we all adjourned to the Cadet Club for hamburgers and beer. After a two-day "honeymoon," our new husbands returned to the base.

Sally and I moved into a two-bedroom converted chicken coop to begin our single married bliss. She was as young and inexperienced as I. We learned, laughed, and coped together. Each afternoon, we rode the bus to the base in time to sign a chit for a hamburger and hold hands (hidden by our skirts) with our new husbands. We repeated this scene every day for a month. Some nights we would all sneak a ride in the back seat of a borrowed car. Finally, the Aviation Cadet Class of 1949 graduated. Sam was a second lieutenant and a jet fighter pilot in the United States Air Force.

My first inkling that this was to be no ordinary life was when Sam happily traded his appointed duty station in safe Biloxi, Mississippi, for duty at Itazuke Air Force Base in Fukuoka, Kyushu, Japan. Our adventure had only just begun. Sam left for Japan in October and once again I was at the mercy of my dear aunts; only this time—thanks to the back-seat car rides—I was pregnant!

I waited, not very patiently, for my order of Port Call. Every day I walked to the post office in this small country town. Everyone in town—all 225—waited to see if I received a letter. They cheered if I did and wished me luck next time if I didn't. Sam called only twice. In our little town there were only party lines, and a telephone call from Japan was an occasion. The military operator would call to inform me I should expect a call from Japan at 2 a.m. These calls were neither satisfactory nor private. As we talked, the line grew fainter and fainter as the community tuned in. Six months after Sam left I received my Port Call. I was on my way, seven thousand miles and seven months pregnant, to be with a man whose face I could hardly remember.

"You must be Carrie," a cheery voice startled me from my reverie and what had become an uncomfortable sleep. The sun was shining brightly through the train window as I realized this stranger had just called my name.

"How do you know me?" I stammered.

She explained her husband was based at Itazuke with Sam. Jim and Sam had discovered we would be on the same train for Port Call. She had boarded the Sunset Limited in Albuquerque, New Mexico.

"But, how did you know who I was?" I asked again.

"Oh," she laughingly said, "that was easy; Jim said you were eighteen and pregnant. Honey, I could not miss you!"

Ginny Lane and I immediately became friends. It was wonderful to talk with someone who had done all this before. A registered nurse, she took charge. We upgraded to a double compartment to be more comfortable and give my growing body some space. Soon I was no longer looking back, but forward to an exciting new life. As Ginny clued me in on the experience of an air force officer's wife, my self-doubt faded, and I looked forward to the future. We watched another beautiful sunset over the Pacific Ocean as we sped along. As morning approached, huge snowdrifts blew from the giant evergreen trees of Oregon. The train straddled high bridges through the mountains and down to the beautiful sea coast of Washington. Two nights and three days after leaving San Antonio, Texas, the Sunset Limited pulled into the Seattle, Washington, station as a gentle rain welcomed us.

An army bus was there to transport military dependents to Fort Lewis for their Port Call to Japan. Ginny and I bunked in a GI (government issue) barrack building with four other wives, all of us eagerly awaiting our departure to Japan. Fort Lewis is an old army base, with pleasant surroundings and beautiful flowers and trees. We spent our days in orientation, physicals, deciphering orders, and anticipating our journey.

2. Air Force Wife 101

Early morning, March 25, 1950, military wives and children boarded the U.S. Navy transport, *General H.B. Freeman*, to Yokahama, Japan. Ginny and I stood on the deck as the ship maneuvered through Colvas Passage, a strait within Puget Sound. Just as the sun began to rise, sparkles formed in the fog. It was a breathtaking sight. I felt a wave of emotion as the shore grew distant and we left our homeland.

Fortunately, Ginny and I were cabin mates. Once out to sea, we inspected the ship and found our cabin. Our eight-by-twelve-foot room had one set of bunk beds, two small closets, and a very small desk. We shared a bathroom with our neighbors. We had a porthole, but it was padlocked. We were on F deck, which I assume was well below water line.

Women with children were separated from those of us considered single. I did not understand this reasoning until I went to G deck to visit Di

Walker, also on her way to Itazuke. Di and her one-year-old baby, Chris Jr., were in a cabin the size of mine with another mother and child. It was hot, children were crying and vomiting, and the odor was very offensive to my pregnant nose. I rushed back to F deck, happy with my lot.

Little time was spent in the cabin. The fresh air on deck was pleasant and helped combat the inevitable seasickness. I was never physically ill—just had that woozy feeling. I never missed a meal, but some poor souls were desperately ill for days and days. I had a crash course in bridge from dear, patient Ginny. According to her, every military wife must play bridge. We visited, walked on deck, and soon became adjusted to life on a moving vessel.

Several days out, a voice boomed on a loud speaker, "Carrie Hawk, report to the dispensary. Carrie Hawk, report to the dispensary!"

Ginny explained that dispensary was the military term for the medical facility. Frightened, not knowing what to expect, I made my way to the dispensary as ordered. A very stern ship's doctor was waiting.

"I was not informed of any pregnant women on board. How far along are you?"

"Seven months," I weakly replied.

"*Good God Almighty*! How did you get on this ship? Regulations are five months and twenty-nine days," he shouted.

I began to sob; this big, important doctor was screaming at me, and I did not know the answer.

He continued, "We are headed into a storm, and I have no provisions for a pregnant woman. You could be knocked against the bulkhead, and your baby could die! *You* could die, and I can do nothing." Still shouting, he dismissed a whimpering, frightened little girl.

As night fell, the wind grew stronger, and the waves began to crash on deck; I was devastated. We had all been ordered to our cabins. Shortly after, there was a knock on our cabin door. There stood a much calmer doctor.

"We are headed into that storm. I brought straps to help hold you in your bunk, and I have ordered meals brought to your cabin until the storm passes." With that he turned and left.

So much for the tough, mean, uncaring doctor!

The storm passed without trauma, my seasickness subsided, and the rest of our days were spent enjoying the sunny deck and playing bridge.

Fourteen days after we said goodbye to America we steamed into Yokohama Bay. About five o'clock in the evening we were all on deck eagerly searching for land when, to our horror, the ship slowed and dropped anchor. We could see Yokohama, we could see figures on the pier, and we knew they were our men. They were only yards of ocean away. We stood on deck and watched the sunset over the bay and the lights of Yokohama burning brightly. Finally, our captain informed us that the Japanese dockworkers had ended their work for the day; we would have to wait until morning to dock. I thought this unusual at the time, but after talking to other arrivals I learned it was SOP (standard operating procedure). We all stood on the deck until we could no longer see movement, and the city lights dimmed. I had never felt so far away—from home and from Sam.

Early, early the next morning, everyone was back on deck. Children's faces were shining. Women who had mournfully lain in bed for two weeks, secluded in their cabins—*everyone* was on deck before dawn in great anticipation. The air was tense as the ship docked at Yokohama pier, and we could see our long lost loves. The pier was brimming with uniforms, straining to find the family so long separated. I was lucky: Sam and a few other second lieutenants were the first to wear the new air force blue uniforms; so among hundreds of pink and green uniforms, these "blue boys" could be spotted easily. I didn't have long to search. There he was, a real live person! No more pictures, letters, or party-line-event phone calls. Suddenly, the ship dropped anchor. I wobbled down the gangplank and into Sam's arms. How safe it was in the arms of Sam Hawk!

After loving kisses and hugs we met Jim and Ginny Lane only to hear what, for me, was devastating news. Jim had been transferred to Missawa Air Base on the northern island of Japan. I thought I could not bear to lose my best friend and caretaker. How would I ever be the perfect air force wife without Ginny Lane? We said a tearful goodbye. Unfortunately, I never saw Ginny again.

3. Japan, a New World

My traveling days were not over. From Yokohama we faced two days and nights on a Japanese train. We made our way to the train station. This was no Sunset Limited. It seemed like a toy train; everything was miniature. The average Japanese person was barely over five feet tall. The seats and bunk beds were made for small people. Before I could settle in, nature called, as it often does with pregnant women. I went swinging and swaying down the small aisle of the rocking train to the rest room. What a shock! The small, unisex room was completely tiled, floor to ceiling. There were no bathroom fixtures. On each wall was a large brass ring, and in the center of the floor was a six-inch square hole. After surveying this situation I realized I was supposed to hold onto the rings and aim at the hole. On a rocking train, squatting while seven-months pregnant and trying to hit a small hole was no easy task. I finally made it back to my seat. Sam laughed 'til he cried; he only regretted the lack of a camera.

"Swinging on the rings!" he chuckled.

Out the window of the train was a completely different world. In the cities as well as the towns bicycles were the preferred mode of transportation. A few miniature Honda cars struggled among the bicycles and *zori*-clad walkers. (*Zoris* are footwear consisting of a slab of wood on two vertical pieces of wood about two inches high. They are held on the foot by a thong. *Zoris* are sometimes worn with foot mittens called *tabis*.)

Our first night together arrived, and I was not about to sleep alone, so Sam and I crawled into a space built for one small Japanese. It took some maneuvering, but we managed—Sam's lanky, six-foot-tall body and my rotund belly with baby *in utero*. We held each other closely as the train rambled past ruins, rice paddies, and towns of Japan.

By morning, we were passing through the ruins of Hiroshima. It was just about five years after the end of World War II, and the results of bombing were still evident. But amid all this devastation was beauty: mountains and rolling hills, perfectly manicured green terraced rice fields, groves of cherry trees, and colorful Shinto shrines tucked serenely into beautiful gardens.

We finally arrived at our destination, Itazuke Air Force Base, Fukuoka, Kyushu, Japan (or *Nippon* in Japanese, which means "source of the sun." This seemed a joke, as it was pouring rain when we arrived, and I soon discovered rain was a frequent occurrence).

4. BOQ 107

There was no officers' housing available. We were temporarily assigned to BOQ 107 (Bachelor Officer Quarters—sans bachelors) to share with another couple. I had met Diane Walker and Chris Jr. on shipboard, and Sam was in the squadron with 1st Lt. Christopher Walker. After introductions, we explored the barracks that would be our home: one common room, four bedrooms, four lavatories, four showers, and—across the hall—four commodes and four urinals. So much for a long-awaited honeymoon! After a few days the guys reported to the flight line.

Di and I were immediate friends with one goal—to turn this male dormitory into a livable, hopefully pleasant home. We hit the *ginzas* of Fukuoka. A *ginza* in 1950s Fukuoka was an outdoor shopping area. Shopkeepers sold pickled vegetables and raw fish soaked in brine and oil from large, open kegs. This combination, along with coal-burning hibachis (small open stoves), and the ever-present incense, reminded me of stale popcorn in San Antonio's Woolworth five-and-dime.

Fukuoka had a couple of department stores; however, American women were not particularly welcome in the business areas. From elevated offices, Japanese men spat down on us. We found this unacceptable, so we spent most of our time in the *ginzas* where shopkeepers were thrilled to get our script (United States military payment certificates that Japanese could exchange for Japanese yen). These poor shopkeepers—trying to make a living after the war—did not care who we were, just that we shopped with them, and we did. We bought cheap silk fabric for curtains, rugs, and of course china, which we found too good and inexpensive to pass up. Later on we found small *mama-san* shops where we could bargain for really good items. In my little world of 1950 Japan, a *mama-san* was a term used to refer to a respected elder, usually a shopkeeper or someone familiar. Armed with our purchases, we began. Industriously we sewed and painted and decorated.

The Japanese furnished maids as a part of a post-World War II reparations agreement. Sam and I were assigned Michiko Ohara, a lovely young woman whose father had been an officer in the Japanese Navy. She was educated and spoke some English. I quickly became attached to Michiko and found her indispensable. Di and Chris were assigned Takane Ashiya, who was also well educated and from an affluent family. Before the war her father had been a college professor. With the help of our maids, BOQ 107 was quickly becoming a home. The question was what to do with four showers and lavatories? The latrine with its four commodes and four urinals was impossible; we shut the door. The shower room had possibilities—we needed a kitchen!

Michiko found a Japanese carpenter, and we went to work. Two shower stalls and one sink close to the hall door were saved for their original intent. We built cabinets over and around the remaining sinks. We kept one sink for washing dishes, clothes, and babies. We went to the BX (Base Exchange) and bought a roaster oven, hot plates, cooking utensils, and dishes. We were in business.

Di and I were very proud of our little home. The common room became a living/dining area with curtains and rugs; and, since Di was an artist, even paintings on the wall! Each couple had a bedroom decorated to their taste. The two other bedrooms were turned into nurseries for one-year-old Chris Jr. and our rapidly approaching baby. Sam and Chris admonished us with every change; Sam, a second lieutenant, and Chris, with a West Point career to protect, were concerned that the United States Air Force would not look kindly on the defacement of military property. Di and I, of course, did not consider our efforts as defacement, but vast improvement. Our solution was to make sure no higher-ranked officers ever darkened the door of BOQ 107. Even after we moved no one ever mentioned the improvements; I often wonder what the future tenants (hopefully not bachelors) thought.

It was five years after the war, and Japan was bankrupt. Families struggled to make ends meet. Fukuoka—in fact all of the island of Kyushu—was very primitive. Everyone walked or rode bicycles or horse-drawn carts. But mostly they walked—in the streets, *en masse*. Men, women, and children scurried in the street. (GIs said that Japanese women had one long side, one topside, and one inside. "GI" was universally used to refer to servicemen.) The majority of Japanese women still wore black kimonos for daily wear. I can still hear the clip-clop of hundreds of *zori*-clad feet.

Great patience was needed to drive in Fukuoka. On advice from Michiko, I learned to hang out the window, beat on the car door, and holler *"Hiarku, isogu, kudasi,"* which means "part, move please." I told Michiko that I did not want to say please or be polite. She insisted that it was the only way.

The narrow, winding road into Fukuoka passed by neatly terraced rice fields heavily traveled by "honey buckets," the GI term for the horse-drawn carts that carried human refuse from the city to the farms and rice patties for fertilizer. Fruits and vegetables were huge, colorful, and off-limits to military personnel. The first months we agreed that it was not sanitary to eat this produce. It was after only a few short months of dried fruit and canned vegetables that we decided the lush red tomatoes were wonderful. We did parboil them and washed them in Clorox water, which we told ourselves would protect us.

One day Michiko asked where I was from.

"Texas," I answered.

Her eyes big as saucers, she ran for Takane. "Madam Carrie from Texas!"

With their broken English and excitement they wanted to know if I had seen a cowboy. I told them my daddy and uncles lived on a ranch, rode horses, worked cattle, and wore boots and Stetson hats. They were amazed; of course, the picture they had of Texas was only from movies. I became their new image of the old West.

Early in June on a bright sunny day, a group of pilots and wives packed a picnic and went to the shore. It was only a few miles from Fukuoka. There we found large white sand dunes and the blue, blue Sea of Japan. It was not easy to walk over the sand dunes, and as I wobbled my pregnant body, I fell—rolling, rolling like a beached whale—down the dune.

Giving birth in a military hospital in a foreign country is quite an experience. Most of the details I'll spare you, but it was a long labor. Sam left for the base while I spent the night alone in a tiny room with one small window. Every once in a while someone would come by and tell me, "Shut up, you have a long way to go."

I kept watching the window for light. Finally, the light came, and so did my beautiful baby. Sam made it back just as she was born.

"Daughter born—both well," Sam announced via Western Union the birth of Bernadette Elaine Hawk.

The doctor was concerned about my roommate, who had delivered twins; her milk had not come in yet. I innocently remarked that I had enough for ten babies. The next thing I knew I was feeding three babies. I pumped for the twins and nursed Bernadette; I was a busy lady for several days.

We took our beautiful red-haired child home to BOQ 107. Even though we were 7,000 miles from home, our new little family was waiting—Di, Chris, Chris Jr., Michiko, and Takane. This baby would not lack for love.

Life settled into a routine, or as much as one can expect with a new baby in the house. We spent a lot of time with Larry and Sally Geropolis, who were also based at Itazuke. The guys were in the same squadron, and since they came together in their new blue uniforms, the older pilots dubbed them "the Gold Dust Twins."

5. War

The shrill blast of sirens disturbed the quiet of the night. Suddenly the telephone rang. Sam sprang to answer.

"Lieutenant Hawk here…yes, sir…yes, sir…right away, sir."

Sam was hurriedly putting on his flight suit while hollering instructions to Chris, who came out of his bedroom, almost naked. A loud speaker was blaring, "Alert…Alert…Alert!"

"What has happened? Where are you going? What should I do?"

An irritated Sam replied, "Help me get my gear together! We have to be at the flight line in fifteen minutes!" The same frantic commotion was going on in the bedroom next door.

Tears in my eyes, and a quiver in my voice, I again asked, "What should I do?"

"Wait for instructions!" Sam replied.

"From whom and how long?"

"Hell Carrie, just wait!"

A swift kiss, and he was gone. I cradled my three-week-old baby in my arms and waited.

Di, Chris Jr., Bernadette, and I huddled together. Di, the daughter of an army general and a military wife for years, had no idea what was going on, either. Was it an emergency or was it a practice run? About daybreak, a jeep with a loud speaker came through our area telling us to stay inside and wait for instructions. Still we waited.

It was June 25, 1950; the Peoples Republic of Korea (North Korea), supplied and advised by China and the USSR, had invaded the Republic of Korea (South Korea). The United Nations, with the United States as principal participant, joined the South Koreans. We were at war. I have been admonished many times for referring to this conflict as a war instead of a police action, because our Congress did not formally declare war. For those of us who lived with our families two hours from the combat zone, whose husbands flew to kill or be killed everyday, and who knew the tales of bravery and death, it was *war.*

In the beginning, pilots in the 35th, 36th, and 80th Fighter Squadrons of the 8th Fighter Group at Itazuke flew cover for transport planes bringing Americans based in Korea to Japan safely. Everyone thought it was just a fracas and would soon be over. Suddenly everything changed. Enemy ground forces began firing at US planes. Chris and Sam were on the floor of BOQ 107 studying gunnery manuals; neither of them had ever fired live guns. Now, cadets have gunnery school as part of their training, but that was not the case in 1950. It was a frantic scene, which frightened Di and me even more. The mission had turned from escort to combat.

All dependents were assembled in the movie theater for instruction on living in a war zone and living with warriors. The base commander reminded us that our husbands were in battle every day. When they were at home, life should be peaceful and relaxed—no arguments, no problems. He made very clear that if we could not cooperate, the government would send us home. I took him at his word and did everything I could to make life easy for Sam. Consequently, I spent the next forty years married to a very spoiled man.

The F-80 jet aircraft had never flown in combat before, and so the first missions were unknown territory. We lost seven pilots the first week of war, including our squadron CO (commanding officer), who had been like a father to the young pilots and to us all.

June 26, 1950

Dearest Folks,

I thought I'd better write and give you the straight scoop. I know you are hearing all sorts of rumors. By the time you get this, it probably will have blown over. Right now the Korean situation is a pretty tricky business. We are only 350 air miles from Korea, so Itazuke is the processing base for dependents, etc., leaving there.

I don't know much except Sam took off on a pre-dawn flight at 5:00 a.m. It's rumored they are flying escort for the big planes flying dependents and army personnel from Korea. Sam can't tell me anything. I just listen to rumors, which is worse than knowing the truth.

There is no use fibbing, I'm scared. I'm all right here. I don't think anything will come of all this, but I hate Sam's being in the middle of it. This base is really alive. They have 1,500 cots set up in the hangars to house the incoming people. The airmen are all on alert, which means they cannot leave the base and must be ready for duty at all hours. I wish I knew more about it all. I am sure it's not as bad as people say. You know how people panic when something like this happens. I hope I haven't alarmed you. I'm all right, and Sam is as calm as can be. He just laughs at me for worrying, so maybe it's not so bad. I had better go to bed. Sixteen-hour working days are tough. Sam is already asleep; he was dead tired, especially under a strain. He acts calm, but I can tell he is on edge. If I have said anything you haven't heard on the news, please don't repeat it, I don't think I have.

Love, Carrie

6. First Martini

One evening, a few weeks into the war, all pilots and wives were invited to the Officers Area Club in Fukuoka. This was a big deal, and I was very excited. It was my first party as a military wife. The purpose of the party was to introduce us to our new commanding officer. This event was the first of what became typical evenings. We drank, sang songs of death and dying, and we drank some more. I was only eighteen, a new mom, and not an experienced drinker. I had never tasted the sophisticated drink called martini, and that night I had three. I proceeded to tell our new CO that my Sam was the "best damned fighter pilot in the air force," and he had been in the army and knew everything about the war. It was time for Sam to take me home.

By the time we made it home that night I was a hopeless drunk. Finding it necessary to hide my baby tummy, I had chosen to wear a Playtex girdle. In 1950 Playtex girdles were made of rubber with breather holes. Kyushu, the southernmost island of Japan, has weather that is very tropical, steamy, and hot in summer. In this atmosphere, Sam endeavored to remove the girdle and put me to bed. I had perspired until my skin had popped out the little breather holes. Poor Sam tugged and pulled, cussed and fretted, until he finally cut the damned thing off. Unfortunately, that wasn't the end of the story: One week later Colonel Davis, the commanding officer, sent Sam to Korea as a forward controller, a ground job that no hotshot fighter pilot wanted. Sam insisted that he was chosen because I talked too much and flirted with the colonel. I don't think that was the reason, but it made for a good story for many years.

Lady in Red
(Tune: "She's More To Be Pitied Than Censured")

'Twas a cold winter's evening, the guests were all leaving,
O'Riley was closing the bar,
When he turned and he said to the lady in red,
"Get out, you can't stay where you are."
She wept a sad tear in her bucket of beer
As she thought of the cold night ahead.
Then a gentleman dapper came out of the crapper,
And these are the words that he said:

"Her mother never told her
The things a young girl should know
About the ways of air force men
And how they come and go (and mostly go).
Now age has taken her beauty,
And sin has left its sad scar.
So remember your mothers and sisters, boys,
And let her sleep under the bar."

7. On the Edge

An unhappy Sam flew to Seoul, Korea, and joined an infantry platoon. It was a two-week mission, and in my naiveté I thought he would be safe. We of course had no communication during this time. Two weeks had passed, and no word from Sam. "Don't worry, Sam's OK," was what I repeatedly heard; however, as days passed, I began to worry. Finally—almost a month after he left—he returned, and I found out that he had been trapped behind enemy lines and rescued just as I was about to receive a missing-in-action visit.

On an air force base during wartime civilian services are not a priority. Consequently, our commissary goods were limited, and our BX was also curtailed, which we all understood. The dispensary was closed except for emergencies. Seeing the nearest doctor for a postnatal exam required a two-day trip on a Japanese train. Instead I chose to read a popular book by the noted pediatrician, Dr. Benjamin Spock, and depend on

Di for advice. Fortunately, I was a young healthy woman with a healthy baby

The Red Cross quickly organized their war effort. They asked for volunteers, and most of the lonely wives participated. My first job was helping at the blood bank. With more and more wounded coming into the 118th Hospital in Fukuoka, the need for blood was imperative. We served juice and cookies to the blood donors after they had finished giving blood. Most of them were glad to get refreshments, especially the cookies, which we often baked in our own ovens. One day a big macho sergeant finished his donation, and I asked him to join us for homemade cookies and juice. He insisted that he didn't need that stuff, but about that time he fainted—crumpled into a ball. Even the toughest need a little pick-me-up after giving blood. I wasn't allowed to give while I was breast-feeding. I remember being disappointed, thinking that was at least something I could do.

Soon, Air Evacuation planes were bringing wounded to Itazuke. Those not seriously wounded were sent to the hospital at Fukuoka. The more serious were on their way to Yokohama or stateside. We met these aircraft with Red Cross chewing gum, candy, etc. At first it was very depressing to see so many broken bodies bandaged everywhere and faces of pain and fear. We were mostly young women, and we talked to them to try to lighten their day. One baby-faced GI asked,

"What is a pretty young thing like you doing in this God-forsaken hole?"

I told him I was married to a pilot flying combat in Korea.

"Why is he fighting this war? He should be home screwing you!"

They all whooped and hollered. At least it took their minds off the pain for a few minutes. It was odd: My depression turned into admiration and even pride that these young men were so brave, although most of them had no idea why they were in battle. They had joined the air force and army and marines, and they were doing their job. Most of them felt being wounded was a failure on their part. As the fighting intensified we had fewer and fewer Air Evac ships. The wounded were more numerous and their wounds more severe, causing them to be flown directly to Yokohama and Tokyo.

Once again sirens blew, phones rang, and loud speakers roared instructions. Hundreds of women and children crowded into waiting buses. All dependents were instructed to report, and we followed orders. North Korean fighter planes had been sighted over the Sea of Japan; we were under a threat of attack. Di and I found seats on one of the buses. We sat quietly and held our babies.

It was a frantic scene, children were screaming as their animals were taken from them. A neighbor, Annie, refused to get on the bus without her little dog. She and her pup went home. We sat on the bus for what seemed like hours; we never moved. Finally, the siren sounded, and we were dismissed. As usual we waited and followed orders—the military way! When we got back to the BOQ area, there sat Annie on her little stoop—drink in one hand, dog Daisy in the other, and a flight helmet on her head. She had handled the alert better than any of us. Several hours later, still shaken, I was nursing Bernie, smoking a cigarette, and drinking a highball. Sam came home, and our first marital fight ensued. How dare I smoke and drink while nursing his child, shame on me! There were several alerts in succeeding months, but none quite as dramatic as the first.

After the alert and the bus fiasco, Sam and Chris suggested Di and I scout the abandoned caves in the hills surrounding Itazuke (probably used as protection when the bombs began to fall on Japan). We gave this some thought. This conjured up the mental picture of the two of us pushing baby carriage and stroller, carrying diapers, bottles, jars of baby food, blankets, pans, and brooms, etc., to clear out such a place. Then there were the varmints we were likely to meet. We became hysterical with laughter and decided perhaps the bus was not such a bad deal after all.

Canteens were set up on the flight line to offer coffee, candy, cold drinks etc., to the pilots returning from combat missions. Dependent wives took turns working at the canteen. When Bernadette was a tiny baby I did not participate, but when she was older I was comfortable leaving her with Michiko. One day, while I was at the canteen, sirens started blaring, and fire trucks and ambulances roared out to the end of the runway. I had seen a flyby formation that Sam flew in, but I had never known exactly which plane was his. We all got as close to the runway as possible. A crew chief in the crowd told us it was Pukin' Pup "Big Zip." That was Sam! He had taken flack in his engine and was making a dead-stick landing. My heart was in my throat, I could not breathe. I tried desperately not to faint. I had to see what was happening, no matter what. He landed safely, and the fire engines and ambulance raced to him. A truck pulled him to his squadron tarmac. He deplaned to cheers of his fellow pilots. I didn't see him until that evening; he was appalled that I had seen what he considered an embarrassment. We never mentioned it after that evening. I decided after that episode that the flight line was no place for me!

(In the Air Force Aviation Cadet program, as in most military schools, the upper classmen are responsible for the discipline of the new cadets, the lower classmen. To accomplish this they participate in various forms of harassment. For some minor infraction Sam was asked to stand in a trash can for hours and repeat a prepared speech about a Zipadeen, the lowest form of humanity known to man. He could recite this spiel verbatim for years. When we were dating, he teasingly called me a Zipadeen. It became his affectionate nickname for me and was eventually shortened to Zip. He chose to name his aircraft Big Zip.)

When Bernadette was four months old she began projectile vomiting, which frightened us all. As a result of a visit to the doctor I discovered that my milk had turned to water; I had to quit nursing my baby. I was brokenhearted. Stress was the diagnosis, and there was no reason to think it would go away. We managed; however, it was not easy. We had only powered milk on base, so we mixed canned milk with boiled water and a little Karo syrup. Bernadette gained weight and grew rapidly. We spent most of our time boiling water, boiling bottles, boiling diapers—boil, boil, and boil. Thank God for Michiko!

The war was everywhere. A pilot friend who lived right behind us was killed. Di and I took turns staying with his wife. It was not very pleasant duty, but we knew our friends would do the same for us.

We had some light moments: Bob Hope came to Itazuke to entertain the troops. A cocktail reception was held for field-grade officers (colonel, lieutenant colonel, and major) and their wives. Sam was a second lieutenant and, of course, not included. One of Bob Hope's pilots, a friend of Sam's, invited us, insisting that no one would notice—famous last words. We dressed in our finest and furtively joined the festivities. We had not been there long when an authoritative voice announced:

"Lieutenant Hawk, are you aware this reception is for field-grade officers only?"

Before Sam could answer, Bob Hope said, "Colonel, leave these kids alone; I invited them!"

Stunned, we tried to thank Mr. Hope, but he just waved us off. We were #1 fans forever!

Several days later Bob Hope and Marilyn Maxwell visited the 118th Station hospital in

Fukuoka. A friend of ours had been shot down and wounded. I do not know the details of his injuries; only that he had some stitches on or around his penis. Hearing this, Marilyn Maxwell crawled into his bed and began to kiss and snuggle him while Bob Hope, doctors, and nurses roared with laughter. With Bob Hope, in addition to Marilyn Maxwell, were the McGuire Sisters, Jerry Colona, and Les Brown and his Band of Renown. Later, Al Jolson entertained; it was a good show, but not quite as memorable as the Bob Hope Tour.

Di and Chris's permanent quarters became available, and they and Takane moved. It wasn't long after that our quarters were available. We were either lucky or Sam knew someone on the Housing Board, because the next available housing was field-grade quarters. Michiko and I packed up Bernadette and our meager belongings and moved into our spacious new home with a real oven, refrigerator, a really nice bathtub, and one commode!

Sometimes the war would almost seem routine and then something would happen to remind us we were fighting with real guns. The door opened, and I heard Michiko scream. Sam was standing there with a bloody silk map wrapped around his arm, and blood running down his face. I didn't have time to faint; Sam was issuing orders: Get this, get that, take me to the hospital in Fukuoka. Instead of going to the hospital first, he had chosen to come home for me rather than have the Death Parade come tell me he was injured. I will always be grateful for that. His plane had been hit by enemy flack, and its windshield had shattered. Pieces of flack and glass were in Sam's arm and one eye. Doctors removed the glass and sent him home. He returned to duty the next morning and was reprimanded for having had his sleeves rolled up.

(Eleven years later, Sam's arm became swollen, and pieces of metal oozed out. It was a grim reminder of a war almost forgotten.)

The monsoon season came with a vengeance. I am from South Texas, where rain is a welcome, but rare, occurrence. When it started raining in the summer of 1950, it seemed to last forever. In those days we hung our cloth diapers outside on a clothesline to dry, along with all the rest of the laundry. Not being able to dry diapers outdoors was a real challenge. We had diapers hanging from every possible bedpost and chair rail, not to mention a few in the oven. I was amazed at the acceptance of the Japanese people. They continued their daily routine, hardly noticing the rain. They crowded the streets, rode their bikes, and drove the honey buckets just as usual and without protection from the water running down their necks.

Day after day, night after night it rained. The war went on, and I worried about Sam flying in all this inclement weather. He insisted he was flying one of the world's newest aircraft with modern instruments. After weeks of rain, doom and gloom, the sun began to peek out once in a while, and suddenly the earth began to steam. The rain was gone, and the hot sun was there. Boy! Did we complain; what we needed was a little cool rain!

July 4, 1950

Dear Folks,

Sorry I haven't written. I don't do much of anything but sit by the radio and listen for news. I do try to sleep during the day. Our hours are so crazy. Sam doesn't get home until 10:00 p.m. or later and up at 4:00 a.m. I get up with him to cook a good breakfast. It's usually his best meal of the day. At least the baby is sleeping through the night. For a while I was nursing her in the latrine so we wouldn't wake Sam. I really wasn't getting any sleep then, but I can't complain. Poor Sam is so tired, he can hardly move.

Things don't look good; yesterday another close friend was killed, two are missing, and one is in the hospital. I just keep praying Sam will be safe. By the way, if you hear about an air raid on Itazuke, it was a false alarm. It scared us all to death but nothing more.

Would it be all right if we send our bonds home for you to put in the lock box? I may send my silver home, too. They have advised us to send home any valuables. If we should have to evacuate we could not take anything with us.

Please excuse the stationery, it is all we have at the BX, and it is rationed along with most things. The ships are being diverted to the war effort.

Rumors are flying that they are going to send dependents home. Our base CO said if he had his way we would all be gone, but orders have to come from General McArthur. I really don't want to leave Sam, but I guess I owe it to Bernadette if things get that bad to keep her safe. If the war continues we can come home after Sam has fifty combat missions; he has twenty now.

I've only been here four months, and I'm as homesick as can be.

Love to all, Carrie

Air Force 801
(Itazuke Tower)
(Tune: "The Wabash Cannonball")

Itazuke Tower, this is Air Force 801,
I'm turning on the downwind, my prop is overrun;
My coolant's overheated, the gauge says 1-2-1,
You'd better get the crash crew out and get them on the
        run.
        (****radio static sound effects****)

Listen, Air Force 801, this is Itazuke tower,
I cannot call the crash crew out, this is their coffee
        hour!
You're not cleared in the pattern, now that is plain to see,
So take it once around again; you're not a V.I.P.
        (* * * * radio static sound effects * * * *)

Itazuke tower, this is Air Force 801,
I'm turning on my final, I'm running on one lung,
I'm gonna land this Mustang, no matter what you say,
I've gotta get my charts squared up before that judgment
        day.
        (* * * * radio static sound effects * * * *)

Now listen, Air Force 801, this is Itazuke tower,
We'd like to let you in right now, but we haven't got the power.
We'll send a note through channels and wait for the reply.
Until we get permission back, just chase around the sky.
        (* * * * radio static sound effects * * * *)

Itazuke tower, this is Air Force 801,
I'm up in pilot's heaven; my flying days are done,
I'm sorry that I blew up; I couldn't make the grade.
I guess I should have waited 'til the landing was okayed.

8. The Death Parade

Morning briefing was at 0500 hours (5:00 a.m.). Pilots received their missions, and briefing lasted about an hour. It took another hour to ready the plane. Take-off was about 0800 hours. F-80 fighter jets fueled for about 2-2.5 hours of combat. Around 1000 hours we would start listening for their return. They flew in four-man formations, and every wife knew the roar of those formations. We would run outside to check the sky. Each squadron had an insignia and color. Sam was in the 36th Fighter Squadron, "The Pukin' Pups." Their plane tails were red. Each day I checked the sky for red tails and four-man formation. If one man was missing from their formation, I usually went to bed and covered my head until I got the "I'm home" call. If someone didn't make it, we would wait for the inevitable "Death Parade": three blue air force sedans, the base commander, the squadron leader, the base chaplain, and the wife's best friend. We would slowly peek out the window and hold our breaths and pray, "Dear God, don't stop here," over and over. Soon the phones would ring,

"They are on A street, C street, turning on 5th street." Finally, I could breathe. It was terrible; I felt such relief and thankfulness that it wasn't my time and yet devastated for my friend who was hurting. If I wasn't needed, I just sat and held my baby.

One day, I got the call from the chaplain. Chris had been shot down. He was alive but seriously injured. When his plane crashed, Chris had been propelled through the cockpit. He was immediately being flown to Tokyo and on to the United States. It was one of my worst days watching my dear sweet friend hear such devastating news. It took Di several days to pack, and then we had to say a very sad farewell. While helping Di, I answered the telephone to find myself talking to Gen. Lawton Collins, Chief of Staff of the Army. In the military, the Joint Chiefs of Staff are real celebrities! I stuttered and stammered and finally managed to give the call to Di. General Collins was Di's godfather. He was a great help getting Di home quickly and the best care at Walter Reed for Chris. Chris spent months in the hospital and years in rehabilitation, I don't think he ever flew again, but it is certain his virility was not damaged; he and Di had eight beautiful children.

The war was not going well; the three fighter squadrons had lost so many pilots, the decision was made for the 36th Squadron to fly F-51 fighters. The F-51 was a prop (propeller) aircraft and a proven workhorse in air-to-ground combat. Sam was strictly an F-80 jet pilot, and he was transferred to the 80th Fighter Squadron, the Headhunters. Most of his buddies were transferred with him, so it was not terribly traumatic; although, as a matter of fact, Sam and the other pilots had always wanted to fly the F-51, because it was real "stick and rudder" flying.

Sam's roommate in basic training, R. B. Crab, was based in Okinawa. He was another hotshot fighter pilot who flew to war with great enthusiasm. R. B. visited us just before the war started, to meet Bernadette and tell us he was in love with my best friend in San Antonio; they planned to marry. We had a wonderful visit, reminiscing about those crazy cadet days, all those double dates. We received news that R. B. was shot down and killed in Korea. R. B. was the best friend Sam had ever had; I had never seen Sam so utterly devastated. We held each other for a very long time. Then, as usual, we dried our eyes, put on our brave faces, and headed to the club for more drinks of forgetfulness and songs of death and dying.

Boozin' Buddies
(Tune: "Wrap Me Up in My Tarpaulin, Jack")

A young jet pilot lay dying;
The medics had left him for dead.
The girls gathered 'round him were crying,
And these are the words that he said:

"Take the tailpipe out of my stomach,
Take the turbine out of my brain,
From the small of my back, the compressor,
And assemble the unit again."

For we are the boys who fly high in the sky,
Bosom buddies while boozin'.
We are the boys that they send out to die,
Bosom buddies while boozin'.

Up in headquarters they sing and they shout,
Speaking of things they know nothing about;
But we are the boys who fly high in the sky,
Bosom buddies while boozin'.
We're the boys that they send out to die,
Bosom buddies while boozin',
Bosom buddies while boozin'.

Sept. 16, 1950

Dearest Folks,

I had another scare last week. It was past time for Sam to be home from the flight lines, so I called operations. They told me he had to make a forced landing in Ashiya (about 30 miles away), and he wouldn't be home until morning. I called Larry and he got more information for me. Sam was all right and got home about 2:00 a.m. He had gotten too low on fuel to make it to Itazuke. It's scary to think he was so low he couldn't make it 30 more miles. Many more scares like that, and I'll be in a straight jacket!

I'm all settled in our new home. We have three bedrooms, living room, dining room, and a wonderful kitchen with a great oven. I have been baking every day.

Auntie, I enjoy your weekly letters so much. They keep me from getting even more homesick than I am. I thought I could come over here for two years at least before becoming homesick, but I've only been here six months, and I'm lonesome to see you all.

Sept. 21

As you can see, I had to stop my letter. Sam came home sick. The flight surgeon grounded him for fatigue. He has slept for three days— only waking for meals! My job is to keep the baby quiet!

I'll close for now. Keep those letters coming.

Love to all, Carrie

9. The Aussies

In October, the 8th Fighter Group was deployed to Seoul; with a couple of hours' notice, we kissed our guys goodbye, held stiff upper lips, and pretended to be brave. Itazuke Air Force Base quickly became a ghost town. The pilots of all three squadrons, their crew chiefs, ground crew, and commanders were all gone. The BX was short on goods, and even the Commissary was short of food—good things like canned soup, Spam, and powered milk! Hundreds of women and children sat by the radio and listened to Armed Forces Radio for news of the war. We played a lot of bridge and canasta and developed hobbies. I had purchased an 8-mm Kodak Movie Camera, which was the latest thing in 1950.

Of course, Bernadette was my favorite—in fact, only—subject. I took pictures of her in her swing, in her bath, in her crib, with friends, with Michiko, with anyone or anything I could get to pose. I learned to splice and edit film. I found a small titling set and went to work. I spent hours putting together film. It has now been transferred to video for my children's families.

Suddenly everything changed, the streets were alive with jeeps, the Officers Club was humming. The Aussies had arrived. The Australian fighter pilots were everything we had heard they were; they jauntily walked with a swagger, with long scarves wrapped and flowing. They were loud, hard-drinking daredevils. They were just what a group of war-weary, lonesome wives needed to spice up our lives. And the rumors and tales of their escapades entertained us all for a while.

One such tale spread like wildfire: A field-grade officer's wife went to the club to see what all the commotion was about. Of course, this good-looking, high-spirited fly guy convinced her to have a drink, and one led to several. She continued to tell him how lonely she was, and how she wanted to see her husband. In their state of impaired judgment, they schemed to fly her across the Sea of Japan for a brief visit with her husband. In an Australian Air Force airplane, they landed in Seoul, Korea. They were ordered to immediately return to Itazuke in secrecy. Another version was that they were never given clearance to land—either way it amused us a great deal. The gossip continued: When the errant wife arrived home she found a note on her pillow, "*Madam joto nai*" (Madam no good). Her houseboy had expressed his opinion.

You Can Tell a Fighter Pilot
(Tune: Battle Hymn of the Republic)

By the ring around his eyeball, you can tell a bombardier;
You can tell a bomber pilot by the spread around his rear,
You can tell a navigator by his sextants, map, and such,
You can tell a fighter pilot, but you cannot tell him much!

Glory, Glory Hallelujah!
Glory, Glory Hallelujah!
Glory, Glory Hallelujah!
You can tell a fighter pilot, but you cannot tell him much!

10. Fukuoka Excursions

It was not long until even the flamboyant Aussies became tiresome. Every day we heard of another of our pilots killed or missing. We all tried desperately to find ways to take our minds off of the war. My diversion was trips into Fukuoka and to *mama-sans.*

Mama-san was a diminutive Japanese lady of undetermined age who had a small shop of treasures: porcelain, Imari bowls, chargers, ivory figurines, brass hibachis, silk brocade kimonos, and a myriad of beautiful ware to take one's mind off the worrisome events of the day. *Mama-san* would trade almost anything for a bottle of rum, and for a rum cake she would give away the shop. Hence, most of my goodies!

One day, one of these trips turned into a small disaster. Sam's crew chief left his car with me when the squadron went to Korea. It was not particularly new, a Ford, very large by Japanese standards. I borrowed a car seat for Bernadette. In 1950, safety was not of major concern. The little chair was canvas hung by two metal bars, which looped over the passenger seat. In downtown Fukuoka, I stopped at a red light. Just then Bernadette sneezed, and I reached to check her. Unfortunately, I had not put the car in neutral, and as my foot slipped off the brake my large American car jumped right up on a mini, mini Japanese Honda. Immediately, this deserted street was teeming with Japanese screaming, "American, American!" Not long after, the Fukuoka police came. Surprisingly, there was little damage to the Honda and, of course, none to the monster Ford. The victims were screaming in Japanese. I could say a few words—hello, goodbye, get out of my way—but none of these seemed appropriate at the time, and I was frightened. Police escorted my baby and me to the police station, where I tried to convince them that I would pay for any damage and to please let me go home. Suddenly, much to my surprise, a representative from the American consulate walked in. He soothed the Japanese, wiped my tears, and with a few words suggested that I try to be careful driving in Fukuoka. I was much too embarrassed to tell Sam and besides, he was not to have any concerns; however, there are no secrets on a base full of bored women. It wasn't long until my little episode was the main topic of conversation in great detail; in fact, the tale grew to such proportions I'm not sure my story is the exact truth!

Just about the time I was recovering from my Fukuoka fiasco, I had another unhappy experience.

One evening the doorbell rang. Michiko answered, and a man in civilian clothes pushed his way in and demanded a sandwich. I told him this was a private home, and he should go. He insisted this was public housing, and he wanted a sandwich. Something happens when one is faced with perceived danger; my adrenaline took hold, and I took charge. I sent Michiko next door with the baby and, as I stared at the intruder, I called the military police. Much to my horror, I was informed that the officer on duty was not present, and military police could not enter an officer's quarters without the Officer of the Day. I was livid that this drunken stranger had invaded my home, and I had to wait for the OD! I finally made him a sandwich, hoping that he might go, but to no avail. Finally the Air Police came and arrested him, a civilian technical representative.

I was very brave when I felt threatened, but as soon as he was gone I turned into a blithering idiot. When Sam came home and heard the story, he immediately took me to the firing range. I had shot a rifle as a girl, but he wanted me to learn to shoot a .45-caliber pistol. I almost shot my foot off. To appease Sam I kept the gun on my bedside table, never to be touched again. In fact, Michiko refused to even dust the table.

Takane, the housemaid of Di and Chris, was getting married. I accepted her invitation to the wedding with great anticipation. I had heard of Shinto weddings lasting days, with drinks and entertainment. The wedding was in an ancient Shinto temple: simple wood beams for a roof, wooden benches for seating, and a very small, raised altar of wood. Takane did not wear the traditional *shiromuku* (white kimono). She wore a beautiful silk brocade traditional kimono that had been in her family for generations. Her *obi* (sash) was huge and must have been many yards long. The groom wore a traditional black kimono. Takane's brightly colored kimono and headdress were the only color at the altar. The priest spoke the traditional Japanese wedding oration, blessed dried leaves, and ceremonially poured green tea over them. The bride and groom drank, the families drank, and finally they offered the cup to the honored guests.

Shortly, we all left the temple and gathered in the garden for pictures. Takane's family kindly asked us to join in the photos. After the picture taking was over we were anticipating the party. Takane's father approached us, thanked us for coming, expressed how honored they were, and said goodbye. We were obviously not welcome at the festivities. The most disappointing thing was that I had captured the entire ceremony on camera, only to discover no film! Takane did not work on the base after her marriage, and I never saw her again.

Oct. 2, 1950

Dearest Folks,

I'm beginning to think I just wasn't meant to have a husband or be an Air Force wife. Sam is leaving again, this time for a very long time, I am afraid. The Fifth Air Force is moving to Korea. He will be able to come home once a month for maybe five days for the next year or so. I am so disappointed and upset and scared.

By the way, how in the world do I stop a four-month-old from sucking her thumb?

I have to start dinner. I'm trying to cook all Sam's favorites so he will remember.

Remember the guy your college roommate, Nancy, asked about? He is in our sister squadron. He was killed the other day. He was a really nice fellow. Please give my sympathy to Nancy.

Love, Carrie

11. Hot Pecker Flights

The Hot Pecker Flights were our salvation. Every couple of weeks a plane would fly to Itazuke from Seoul on military business. In their great wisdom and sensitivity the COs chose to send married pilots on those missions. It was usually an overnight. When it was our turn we felt like God was smiling on us.

In October, Sam completed fifty combat missions. The original plan was to return stateside after fifty missions, but as always in war, the situation changed. Instead, Sam was given a week of R&R (Rest and Recuperation). We happily packed Bernadette and Michiko and boarded a bus for the Aso Kanko Hotel, a beautiful palace that had been a summer retreat for the Japanese emperor, Hirohito. It was nestled at the foot of Mount Aso, one of the five cone-shaped mountains. It boasted the world's largest volcanic caldera. Below these fuming craters were lush green trails and warm spring waters.

We were given a beautiful suite of rooms. There was an exceptionally large ceramic-tiled bathtub— big enough for both Sam and me—immediately tempting! The tennis courts inspired Sam to teach me tennis, which was a disaster, We settled for a dip in the Aso Kanko warm spring bath. It was a large indoor coed bath, my first experience at coed bathing. Fortunately, at our first visit, we were the only participants sans clothes. The *mama-san* there had to guide us and explain the procedure. We entered the steaming water slowly to acclimate our bodies to the heat. After a while she beckoned us to move to an area covered with wooden slats. She gave us soap to cleanse our bodies, then poured buckets of water to rinse us. Finally, we returned to the large pool to relax. At this point we were given towels and each taken into a small warm room with an *itami* (a straw mat) on the floor for a wonderful Japanese-style massage. After all this, Sam and I were ready for a nap in our nice cool bedroom. I never did get enough nerve to join coed guests in the bath. After several really great days of peace, it was time to return to Itazuke and the war.

Sam immediately flew back to Seoul and the front lines. The war was raging, the Chinese had crossed the Yalu River, and the North Korean mantra was "stand and die." The skies were more dangerous than ever. The Allied forces were being pushed back, and even the Hot Pecker Flights were no longer running. The only news we had came on the radio. The Aussies were gone, and the commissary and BX were bare. The Death Parade still haunted our streets. We all kept smiling— telling each other it would all end soon. We played bridge, smoked several packs of cigarettes a day, bit our nails, and prayed constantly. Everyone was homesick and frightened. We told each other we were brave air force wives, but we cried ourselves to sleep each night.

A friend's husband was killed, and it was especially traumatic for her. She and her husband had fought when he was last home, and she was convinced he had not forgotten. The other wives and I tried our best to convince her that he had long gotten past any problems they had. To add to her trauma, she was informed it was "friendly fire." This is a terrible way for a spouse to encounter death. She went home and joined the many widows there.

Nov. 28, 1950

Dearest Folks,

Well here I am with nothing to say except sad tales of war. Sam is still in Korea, and the allied forces are under stiff opposition. I'm so worried about him that I'm nearly nuts. One of our close friends was killed—one of our closest since Di and Chris left. Harvey was engaged to my friend Bonnie, whose father is stationed here. She is my age, and we have become good friends. Before the guys left Itazuke, we played bridge and shopped at Mama-san's. When death happens to your best friend like Harvey or Di and Chris, it can't help but leave a mark—let alone all the others. I just can't stand much more. I wish he could call me; it would be better, but now every night I worry that he may be scattered on a hill somewhere. All the wives feel the same way, but no one admits it. I guess that's why I'm writing. We all run around acting like brave wives, but none of us is; everyone is as scared as I am. We all bite our nails, smoke too much, yell at our kids, and toss and turn all night; and never stop praying that our men will come home safe.

I want to come home so bad. I want to feel the safety and comfort of my family. I want you to meet Bernadette and for her to know you. But of course I wouldn't come home without Sam for anything in the world. If this damn war ever ends, we are coming home to stay. Sam will get out of the Air Force and go to school. It might be hard, but all the money in the world is not worth living like this.

Auntie, please don't send this letter on to the family. They will worry about me. I'm really all right. I just had to blow off to someone, and you are my sounding board. Sorry. Your Christmas gifts will probably be late. I've been so rattled that I haven't sent anything. Sorry.

Love, Carrie

Korean Waterfall
(Oh Death, Where Is Thy Sting?)

His parachute hung from a nearby tree, he was not quite
    dead;
So listen to the very last words the young jet pilot said:
"I'm going to a better land where everything's all right,
Where whiskey flows from telegraph poles, play poker
    every night.
We haven't got a thing to do but sit around and sing,
And all the crews are women; oh death, where is thy
    sting?"

Death, where is thy sting, ring-a-ling?
Oh, death, where is thy sting?
The bells of hell will ring-a-ling, a-ling
For you! But not for me!

So-o-o, ring-a-ling-a-ling-ling; blow it out your pilot
    tube.
Ring-a-ling-a-ling-ling; blow it out your pilot tube.
Ring-a-ling-a-ling-ling; blow it out your pilot tube.
Better days are coming, bye and bye!

12. Mixed Blessings

By November's end, the Allied forces were pushed back, and the Itazuke-based fighter squadrons returned to their home base. They resumed the daily missions from Itazuke. I had very mixed emotions: Sam was devastated that the war was going badly, and even though the danger was still with us, he was home. I could touch him, take care of him, and make sure he had that great breakfast every morning at 4 a.m. The best part—it was Christmas, and Sam would be home for Bernie's first Christmas. The Commissary surprised us with frozen turkeys. When word got around that turkeys were in, the lines grew long. A big problem was refrigeration; one must not buy too soon, because our refrigerator freezers accommodated only two ice trays. Somehow we managed, and on Christmas Day we had turkey, dressing, and all the trimmings. It was my first holiday dinner, but with the help of Sara, a friend since cadet days, we had a very memorable day; however, the war went on.

****

Dec. 22, 1950

Dearest Folks,

This will be a short note as this is my last piece of stationery, and the BX is out too. They promise some next week, but don't hold your breath! Glory be! I am happier than I have been in a long time. Sam is not happy, but I am. Everything has worked out fine. Sam is home to stay, and he has a cold; so he is grounded, which means he will be home for Christmas!! Bernadette's first will be Sam's and my first Christmas together. I can't help but be happy, happy. I have prayed and prayed for Christmas together, but Sam is mad and miserable.

I've been baking and cooking for days. This is the first Christmas dinner I have ever cooked. We are having friends over. I am petrified but just tell myself I can do this. I wish we could be home with you for Christmas. This is my first Christmas away from you all. My thoughts will be with you and maybe we'll be there next year!

Merry Christmas to all,

Love, Carrie

****

The winter of 1951 was miserable in Japan, and treacherous in Korea; heavy snows and icy conditions made flying difficult. God help the pilot who was shot down; search and rescue were impossible, and survival even less likely. We had one pilot who had to bail out in the snow-covered terrain; he survived, but his feet froze and had to be amputated. Sam, flying with a cold, burst an eardrum and was grounded for a few days. It would have been nice had he not been miserable and angry at the world. His ear healed, and soon he was back to the daily routine of war and death.

By this time nothing helped to forget the terrible events of the daily war. My friend was lost. The North Koreans were flying Russian MiGs, which were a challenge for our fighters. The Air Force brought in F-86 fighter jets to combat the MiGs. Even the toilet paper fights and crazy escapades at the Club couldn't make the hurt go away. The only good news was that we did not seem to have as many casualties as in the beginning—or maybe we had just gotten used to the Death Parade.

March arrived, but one day wasn't much different from the next. The war was dragging on; it was cold, and spirits were low. Even the parties were not fun and were more and more infrequent. Our guys still flew missions every day, and of course there was still danger.

After one particular mission, Sam was unusually distraught, pensive, and brooding. Eventually, after several drinks, he relaxed and shared his day. On strafing missions (machine gun firing from low-flying aircraft) pilots were ordered to fire on all moving objects, no matter how innocent they seemed. The enemy was known to hide arms and military equipment in unconventional modes. This day Sam had encountered and strafed a wagon driven by an old man and woman and pulled by two white horses.

"Killing old men, pregnant women, little children, and beautiful white horses is all this damn war is about," he said.

It was not the first such incident nor the last, but that nightmare stayed with Sam for many years.

Bless 'Em All
(Tune: "Troop Ship Leaving Bombay")

Bless 'em all, bless 'em all,
The long and the short and the tall.
Bless old man Lockheed for building this jet,
I know a guy who is cursing him yet.
For he tried to go over the wall
With his tiptanks, his tailpipe, and all.
The needles did cross, and the wings did come off.
So cheer up my lads, bless 'em all.

Bless 'em all, bless 'em all,
The needle, the airspeed, and ball.
Bless those instructors who taught us to fly,
Sent us to solo, and left us to die.
And if ever your blow jet should stall,
You're in for one hell of a fall!
No lilies or violets for dead fighter pilots,
So cheer up my lads, bless 'em all.

Bless 'em all, bless 'em all,
The long and the short and the tall.
Bless all the sergeants and their bloody sons.
Bless all the corporals, the fat-headed ones.
For we're saying goodbye to them all,
The long and the short and the tall.
Here's to you and lots others, you can shove it up,
    brothers;
We're going back home in the fall!

13. Hallelujah!

Suddenly it happened; Sam came home with orders for stateside, and—best of all—they had grounded Sam. He had 125 combat missions, and I guess his commanding officer was afraid his luck had run out. He was through with the Korean War. He was unhappy because the F-86s and MiGs were meeting in dog fights every day, and lots of his buddies were becoming jet aces (five kills). That was what Sam wanted more than anything. I was so happy; it annoyed me that he wasn't as excited as I. In later years, I realized what a disappointment it was for him. He had four Distinguished Flying Crosses and other service awards, but he wasn't an ace. Later in the war, several of his friends became triple aces.

Sam always regretted what he considered his failure, but Oh God! I was delirious! I started packing and planning right away. Time passed slowly, but finally the day arrived. Our squadron gave us a rousing send-off with hugs and promises to keep in touch forever. We boarded a C-47 for Tokyo. We spent three days in the Imperial Hotel; I guess it was nice, and we have pictures of Tokyo that look interesting, but honestly all I wanted was to go home. Finally Sam and I and ten-month-old Bernadette, five other couples, and a few single airmen boarded a USAF Constellation (nicknamed The Connie). It was a slow-flying boxcar, but it was taking me home. A few hours out we hit rough weather, and Bernadette vomited all over the beautiful wool tweed suit I had made especially to wear home—not thinking it was March, and I was going to Texas. I cleaned us up as well as I could, and our journey continued.

We landed on Wake Island. I was surprised that it was so small; so many men were killed trying to protect this tiny little island. It was dark, but the fresh air felt good. It seemed that we walked all the way around the island; then we were off again. On this leg of the trip Bernadette developed diarrhea. Those were the days of cloth diapers. Poor baby, she had a diaper rash that hurt, an airsick tummy, and a stinking diaper. Trying to maintain some sort of sanitary conditions sitting in a seat of a military aircraft was not a simple matter.

After what seemed like days, we reached Honolulu. Not only was Bernadette a mess, I was in a wool suit that had been severely impaired. I'm sure our fellow travelers were as glad to get some fresh air as we were. Just then angels appeared; they were Red Cross workers, but they looked like angels to me. They took Bernadette and insisted that I shower and get into fresh clothes. Then they promised to take care of my baby while Sam and I had a lovely dinner in a wonderful restaurant by the beautiful ocean. When we returned, our baby was bathed and in clean clothes; those dirty, smelly diapers had been replaced. God bless the Red Cross!

Throw a Nickel on the Grass
(Tune: "Throw a Nickel on the Drum")

I was lyin' in the gutter, all covered up with beer!
Pretzels in my eyebrows, I knew the end was near,
When along came the air force and saved me from the
    hearse.
Glory, Glory, Hallelujah, sing another verse:

Chorus:
Sing Hallelujah! Sing Hallelujah!
Throw a nickel on the grass, save a fighter pilot's ass.
Sing Hallelujah! Sing Hallelujah!
Throw a nickel on the grass, and you'll be saved!

Cruising down the Yalu, doing three-and-twenty per
A call came from a major, "Oh, won't you save me, Sir!
Got flack holes in my wingtips, and my tanks ain't got
    no gas!
Mayday! Mayday! Mayday! Got six MiGs on my ass!
(Chorus)

Shot my traffic pattern; to me it looked all right.
The airspeed read one thirty, I really racked it tight.
The airframe gave a shudder, the engine gave a wheeze.
Mayday! Mayday! Mayday! Spin instructions please!
(Chorus)

14. The United States of America

After long hours, the last leg of our journey home was over. We landed at Travis Air Force Base, San Francisco, *USA*. I would have thrown myself on the ground in delirious joy, but Sam would have left me in the middle of the runway. After all, the returning war hero was much too cool for such demonstrations. We were boarded onto a bus. I prayed, "Oh God, please deliver me from military buses," and He did! We were escorted to a beautiful room at the luxurious, world-famous St. Francis Hotel. I had never been in such luxury. In fact, my naiveté soon reared its inexperienced head. It was late evening; and I was sure little Bernadette was eager to have her bottle in a nice, big, clean, and fresh crib. Not realizing I should call room service, I started out to find the kitchen. I wandered around and found some back elevators and finally found the kitchen. Needless to say, the kitchen workers were more than surprised to find me, with baby and bottle in hand. When I explained that I needed boiled water for my baby, they were very confused. It had not dawned on me that I would never have to boil water or mix canned or powered milk again. Embarrassed, I gained my composure and returned to my room.

The next morning we discovered our life was in civilian hands. We caught a taxicab to the San Francisco Airport to board a TWA flight to Philadelphia (Sam had convinced me that if we visited his folks first, we could stay longer with my family). Off we flew. The flight stewardesses were very kind and attentive. They were impressed that Sam was a pilot returning from Korea. A few hours into the flight, Sam called the stewardess to report a fire in the left engine. She rolled her eyes and muttered that she would tell the Captain. We flew on, and Sam got up to talk with the Captain. Of course the stewardess wouldn't let him, but he made so much noise that I guess the stewardess informed the captain that some nut fighter pilot smelled smoke. A little later the Captain announced that he was diverting to Phoenix because of slight engine trouble. Sam loved it!

We arrived in Philadelphia. Sam's family was there to meet us. I was nervous because I had met them only once, just after we married. I should not have worried; they hardly knew I was there. Sam and Bernadette were all they could see.

One of the most puzzling things to me at the time was what little interest people stateside had in the war. When we visited Sam's old buddies, they seldom asked about the war. Most of them had nine- to thirteen-inch television sets. I had never seen TV, but since about all they watched was wrestling, I was not impressed. Sam and I were so full of the war and had lost so many friends that we wanted Sam's buddies to understand the horrors we had been through, but we all sat in the dark and watched wrestling.

It was finally time to go to *Texas*! Everything went smoothly until we had to change planes in New Orleans. Because we were military we were flying non-revenue (space available). We were supposed to board a Trans-Texas Airways flight to San Antonio, but there was no room for us. I could not believe it—this close and they wouldn't let me on the plane! I lost it! Sam's pride be damned; I stomped my feet and threw a first-class fit. The next flight did not leave until morning, so we had to stay in New Orleans. Under normal conditions that would have been fun, but I was in no mood for fun. The airline gave us a room at a motel near the airport. It was not the St. Francis. They had no crib, so my baby slept in a drawer from the only chest in the room. Early the next morning we arrived in San Antonio and into the arms of my loving family. Life was good.

Epilogue

Jack went on to have twenty-two years in the air force, both active and reserve duty. He flew F-80s, F-86s, and C-130s. He retired as a lieutenant colonel. In 1953 our second beautiful daughter, Jacquelyn, was born at George Air Force Base, Victorville, California. Tragically, our beautiful Bernadette Joy Elaine died of breast cancer at age 39. She gave us wonderful grandchildren. I now have five grandchildren and seven of the most beautiful, most intelligent great-grandchildren, to whom this book is dedicated so they will know what kind of man Jack Rico't was. They knew him as Popo, but he was always, first and foremost, Sam Hawk, fighter pilot.

Jack died November 24, 2007.

Corinne Martin Rico't